Please check all items for damages
before leaving the Library.
Thereafter you will be held
responsible for all injuries
to items beyond reasonable wear.

# 3D Modeling

HELEN PLUM LIBRARY
LOMBARD, IL

CHERRY LAKE PUBLISHING • ANN ARBOR, MICHIGAN

by Theo Zizka

CHERRY
LAKE
Publishing

*A Note to Adults: Please review the instructions for the activities in this book before allowing children to do them. Be sure to help them with any activities you do not think they can safely complete on their own.*

*A Note to Kids: Be sure to ask an adult for help with these activities when you need it. Always put your safety first!*

Published in the United States of America by Cherry Lake Publishing
Ann Arbor, Michigan
www.cherrylakepublishing.com

Series editor: Kristin Fontichiaro

Photo Credits: Cover and page 1, kjarrett/www.flickr.com/CC BY 2.0;
pages 4 and 8, vancouverfilmschool/www.flickr.com/CC BY 2.0;
page 7, Creative Tools/www.flickr.com/CC BY 2.0; pages 9, 11,
13, 14, 16, 18, 20, 21, 23, 25, 29, Theo Zizka; page 15, FHKE/
www.flickr.com/CC BY-SA 20; page 24, fdecomite/www.flickr.com/
CC BY 2.0; page 26, OpenCurso/www.flickr.com/CC BY 2.0; page 27,
4everMiku/www.flickr.com/CC BY 2.0.

Library of Congress Cataloging-in-Publication Data
Zizka, Theo, author.
  3D modeling / by Theo Zizka.pages cm. — (21st century skills innovation library.
    Makers as innovators)Summary: "Learn how to create computer-generate
  3D models like the ones used in video games and animated films" — Provided by
  publisher.Audience: Grades 4 to 6.Includes bibliographical references and index.
  ISBN 978-1-63137-772-3 (lib. bdg.) — ISBN 978-1-63137-792-1 (pbk.)
— ISBN 978-1-63137-832-4 (e-book) — ISBN 978-1-63137-812-6 (pdf)
  1. Three-dimensional imaging—Juvenile literature. 2. SketchUp—Juvenile
literature. 3. Computer graphics—Juvenile literature. I. Title. II.
Series: 21st century skills innovation library. Makers as innovators.
  TA1560.Z59 2015006.
  6'93—dc 23                    2014006970

Cherry Lake Publishing would like to acknowledge the work of The Partnership for
21st Century Skills. Please visit *www.p21.org* for more information.

Printed in the United States of America
Corporate Graphics Inc.
July 2014

# Contents

**Chapter 1**

# What Is 3D Modeling?

**H**ave you ever had an idea for something you wanted to make, but you weren't sure how to make it? Or what it should look like? Have you ever picked up a household object and wondered why it is shaped the way it is? Everything man-made

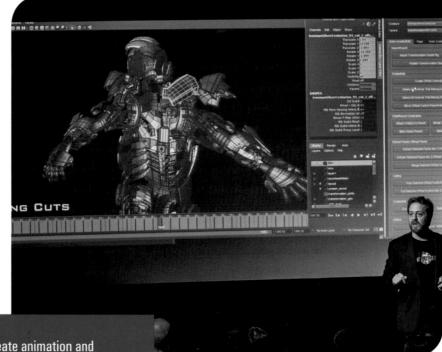

3D models are used to create animation and special effects in movies.

begins as an idea in someone's head. But how does it take on its final form? The answer is modeling.

Modeling has been around for a very long time. Designers, artists, and other **makers** use materials such as clay, wood, and paper to build early versions of their creations. They can observe, measure, and test these models to make sure a final object will work correctly. They can also make sure it will be the right size, shape, and color. However, building physical models can be expensive and time-consuming.

In recent years, makers have relied more and more on 3D modeling computer software to test out their ideas. This allows them to create models quickly and easily. Computer-generated models are also easy to tweak if changes need to be made.

There are three main kinds of 3D modeling. **Polygonal** modeling uses three-dimensional shapes such as cubes or spheres to create models. You can see its results in your favorite video game or animated movie. Curve modeling is based purely on mathematics. It can be used to create models using very precise measurements. This makes it useful for modeling things that will later be built as real-life objects, such as buildings, cars, or electronics.

The newest kind of 3D modeling is called digital sculpting. This type of modeling is a lot like making something out of clay. Makers can pull, smooth, grab, pinch, slice, and poke their models in the software. Like polygonal modeling, digital sculpting is mainly used for computer graphics and special effects. However, it can add more detail than polygonal modeling can.

All three types of 3D modeling allow the user to make **renderings**. A rendering is a picture or video of what the model would look like as a real-life object.

## Modeling and Makers

Makers are creative people who are curious about the way things work. They use a wide variety of skills and tools to build things, take them apart, repair them, and improve them. Makers often gather in places called makerspaces, guilds, clubs, or studios. There, they can share ideas, tools, and skills.

Most makerspaces are equipped with high-end computers and a variety of software that is useful to makers. This often includes 3D modeling software. Some makers rely heavily on this software to help them plan out new inventions. Others use it to create animated films or other digital artwork.

Computer-generated 3D models can be turned into physical objects using 3D printers.

This includes its texture, color, and size. When you pass by an empty lot that is going to be used for a construction project, you might notice a sign with a picture of what the new building will look like. That picture is a rendering. The building does not yet exist physically. It only exists in a computer, on paper, and possibly as a miniature model.

Like learning to play an instrument, mastering 3D modeling software takes time, practice, and a lot of trial and error. Lots of things will go wrong as you learn. But as long as you save your work often, you should be able to recover anything you might have lost.

This book will teach you the basics of curve modeling using SketchUp, a free program that can be downloaded from the Internet. However, most curve modeling is the same no matter what software you use. Knowing how to use SketchUp will help you learn other 3D modeling software.

Mastering the art of 3D modeling takes a lot of practice.

## Chapter 2

# Navigating the Virtual World

To get started in the world of 3D modeling, you will need a computer and an e-mail address. Ask an adult to help you find and download the SketchUp software. At the time of this writing, it can be found at www.sketchup.com/download. The SketchUp Web site will ask what you are going to use the program for. Select Personal Projects and type in your

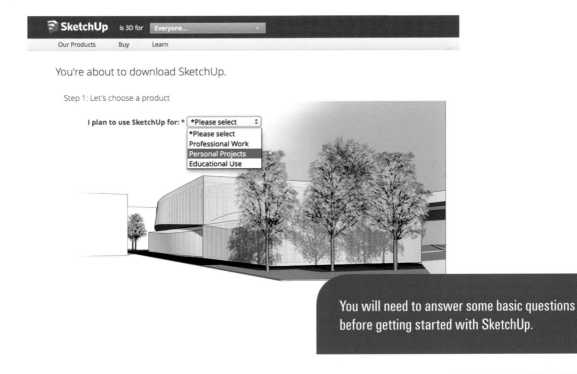

You will need to answer some basic questions before getting started with SketchUp.

e-mail address. The site will now ask you to select your profession. Choose Other.

Once you have downloaded and installed SketchUp, open the program. It will ask you to choose a **template**. Choose Simple. Then click on Start Using SketchUp. You will see three lines called **axes**. The blue one goes up and down. This means it's the vertical axis, or y-axis. The red one goes left to right. This means it's the horizontal axis, or x-axis. The green one looks like it goes left to right, but it actually goes into the screen and out of it. This one is called the z-axis. The point where all of these lines meet is called the origin.

Next to the origin, there should be a picture of a person. Click on it. The lines around the person will turn blue, and a blue rectangle should appear around the person. You have just used the Select tool. The Select tool looks like a computer cursor. It allows you to choose the things that you want to change. When something is selected, it will be out-lined in blue.

Now wave good-bye to the person and press Delete or Backspace on your keyboard. The person will vanish! Don't worry, though. You can undo this or any other action by pressing Command and Z at the same time on a Mac computer, or Control and Z if you are on a Windows computer. This is useful anytime you make a mistake.

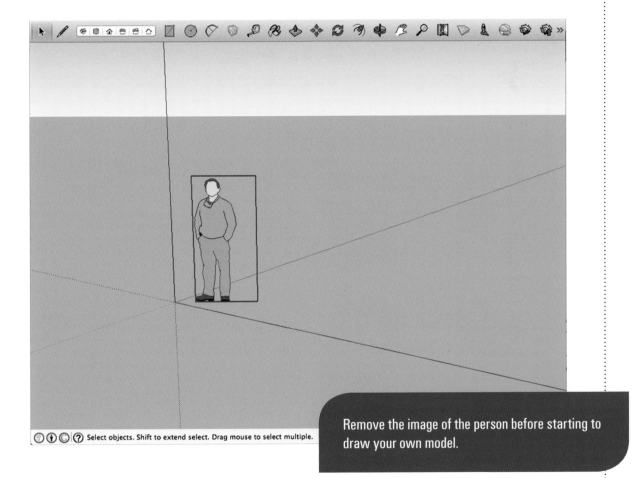

Remove the image of the person before starting to draw your own model.

Let's learn how to use some more tools. There is a line of symbols near the top of the SketchUp window. This is called the toolbar. Each symbol represents a different tool. When you first open SketchUp, it should show 23 tools. There are many more than that, and you can add them to your toolbar when you need them. For now, we only need the basics.

Click on the brown rectangle with a red line through it. This is the Rectangle tool. Go back down to the green plane where the person was standing and click on the origin. It will turn yellow when you get near it. When you move your mouse, the lines of a possible rectangle will form. A dotted, diagonal line will appear if you are about to create a square. The next place you click makes the rectangle, which turns gray. You've just created a surface!

You can't do much with just one surface. However, this surface has possibilities. Go back up to the toolbar and select the box that has an arrow going up. SketchUp calls this the Push/Pull tool. Other programs call it the Extrude tool. It allows you to pull a surface outward or push it inward to give it a new shape. If you put your mouse on the rectangle you made, the gray surface will be speckled with blue dots. This tells you that you can push or pull it. Click, and the rectangle will rise or fall with your mouse movements to form a three-dimensional box.

The box has six sides, but you can only see three at a time. Thankfully, there are tools to help you see the rest of the box. Go up to the toolbar and select the red and green arrows chasing after each other

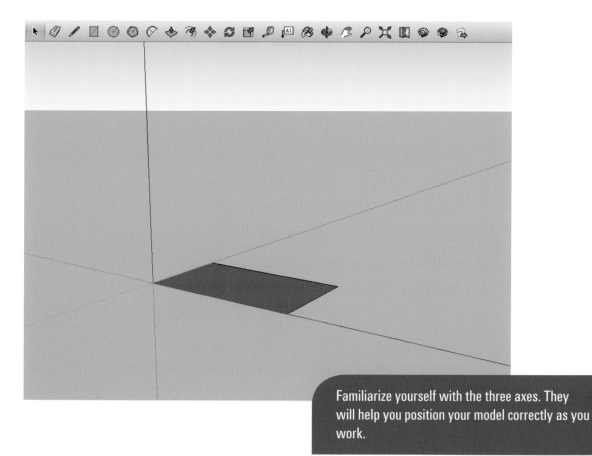

Familiarize yourself with the three axes. They will help you position your model correctly as you work.

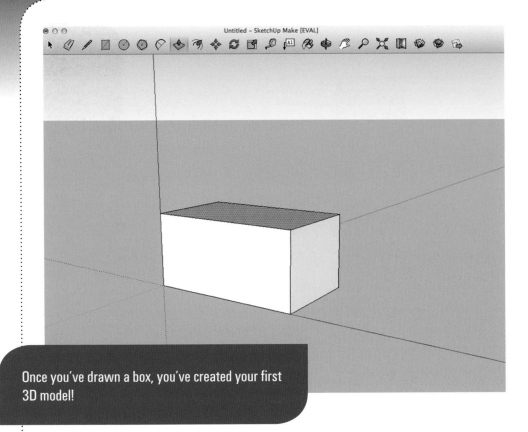

Once you've drawn a box, you've created your first 3D model!

around a pole. This is called the Orbit tool. Go back down to the box. Now you can spin around it by clicking and dragging your mouse. Back on the toolbar, select the hand next to the Orbit tool. This is called the **Pan** tool. When this tool is selected, clicking and dragging allows you to move side to side in front of the object.

The **Zoom** tool is the magnifying glass next to the Pan tool. With this tool selected, clicking and dragging upward will zoom in. Clicking and dragging

**A New View**

Now that you've learned the basics of SketchUp, try putting your skills to the test. Make a second box next to the first one you made. Leave some room in between the two boxes. Can you position your view between the two boxes by zooming, panning, and orbiting? Can you zoom inside a box? If you can do these things, you have mastered the art of moving around a digital 3D space!

downward zooms out. If you have a scroll wheel on your mouse, scrolling toward the computer zooms in. Scrolling away zooms out. Now you know how to move around in a virtual world!

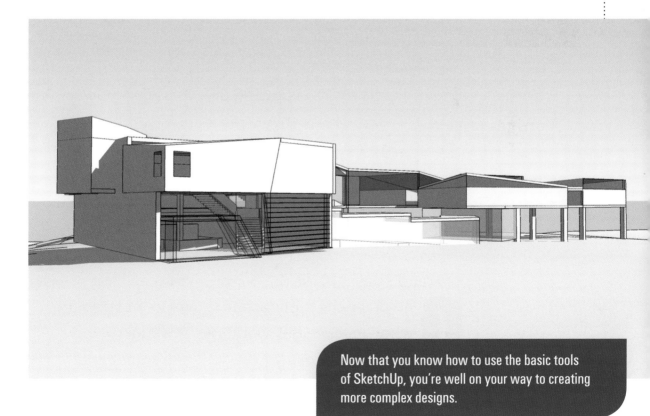

Now that you know how to use the basic tools of SketchUp, you're well on your way to creating more complex designs.

**Chapter 3**

# Putting the "3D" in 3D Modeling

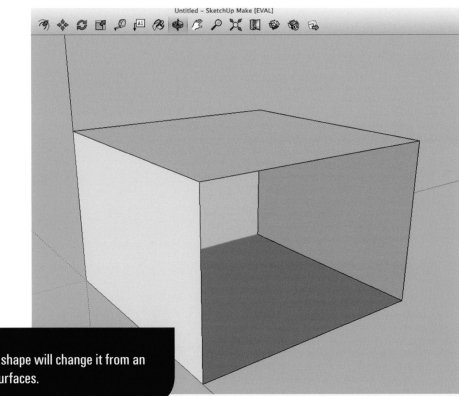

Untitled – SketchUp Make [EVAL]

Removing pieces of a shape will change it from an object to a series of surfaces.

ne of the most important things to understand when modeling is workflow. Workflow is the series of actions you do to make something.

In 3D modeling, the workflow usually starts with the shapes that make up an object's **underlying geometry**. These shapes are then altered to make more complex shapes. In chapter two, the rectangle you drew was the underlying geometry. You then altered it to become a 3D box shape. This box can be further changed in some fun ways, so let's learn about some more tools.

Draw a box by making a rectangle and pulling it up. Now use the Select tool and click on one side of the rectangle. It will turn blue. If you delete that side, the rest of the box will still be there, but the inside will be dark gray. This is important. It means the box is no longer a solid shape. Instead, it is like a paper box without a top. Nothing can be done with this outside of SketchUp. It cannot be turned into a physical object. Therefore, press Control or Command and Z to undo the action. As long as there are no holes in the object, it is a solid.

Go up to the toolbar and select the pencil. This is the Line tool. It allows you to draw straight lines point by point. Go back down to your solid box and click on one of the edges. Then click on another edge. You've created a new surface that can be pushed or pulled into another shape. If you push it inward, you can

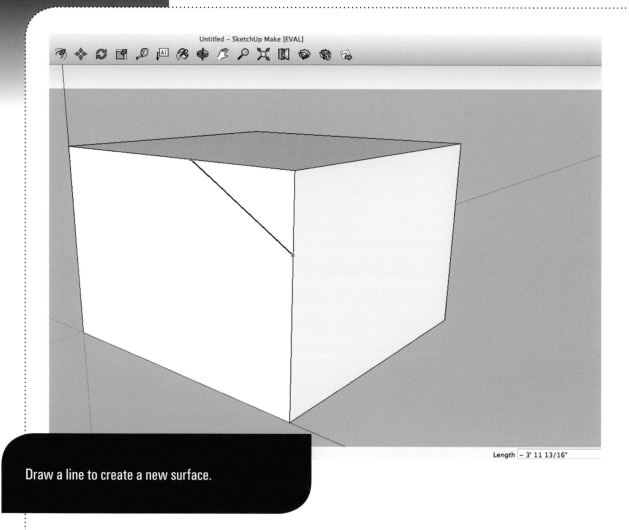

Untitled – SketchUp Make [EVAL]

Length ~ 3' 11 13/16"

Draw a line to create a new surface.

completely get rid of part of the original box. It is like slicing off a piece of an apple.

This doesn't happen with just straight lines. Select the circle with a red **radius** from the toolbar. Now draw a circle on the box and push it through the box to form a hole. Examine the hole you just made. The box is still a solid, even though there's a hole. This is because no surfaces were deleted. Instead, you made a cylindrical surface that connected two sides of the box. Notice that there are no dark gray gaps in the solid.

Now let's add a new tool to the toolbar. Click on the View menu at the top of the screen. Select the Customize Toolbar option. Look at all of those tools! The one we want is the long bar with six views of a house on it. Click and drag that tool onto the toolbar. You can put it wherever you like.

Before we can continue, we need to get rid of the things that are already in the workspace. Choose the Select tool. Now click and drag the mouse to create a rectangle with dotted sides around your model. Everything inside this rectangle will be selected. You can delete, move, or alter it.

Once the area is empty, go up to the new symbols you added to the toolbar. Select the one that's looking down at the roof. It's the second one from the left. The workspace will change. Don't worry. This just means we're looking at it from a different angle. We are looking straight down at the origin. This means it will be easier to draw flat shapes. Now let's spell out "3D."

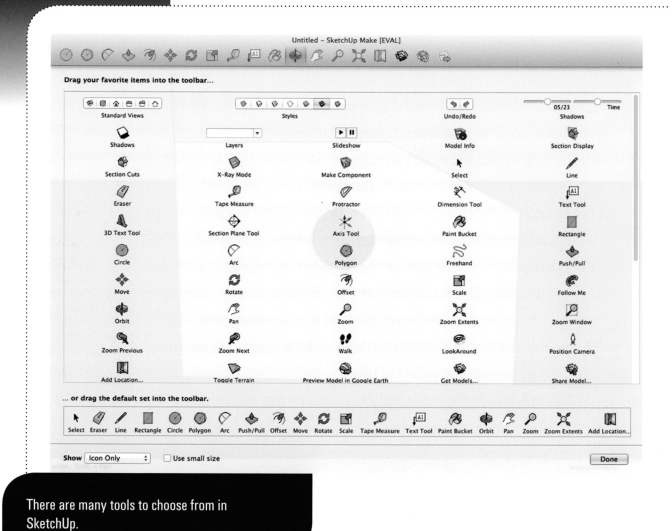

There are many tools to choose from in SketchUp.

Select the Rectangle tool and make the right side of the "3." (We're going to make the number without curves.) Now make another rectangle for the top of the "3." Make two more for the bottom and center lines of the "3." Now use the Select tool to click on the lines between each of the rectangles. Delete each line. This will connect the four rectangles into a single shape.

Next we'll draw the "D." Use the Rectangle tool to draw the left side of the "D." Now let's use a different tool called the **Arc** tool. It is the one to the left of the

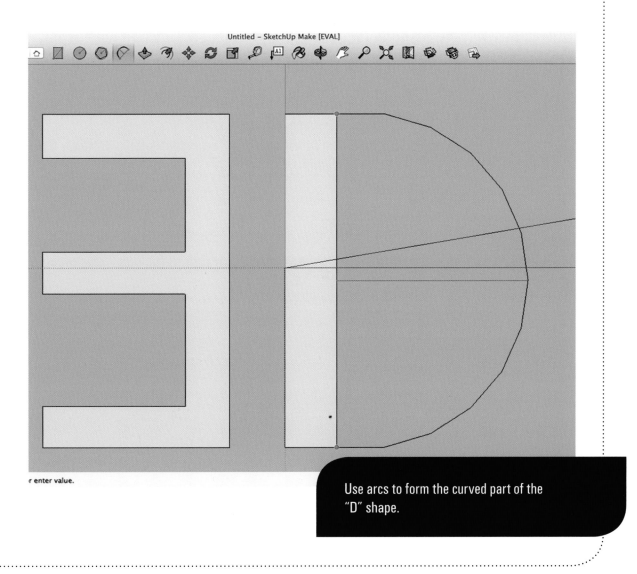

Untitled – SketchUp Make [EVAL]

r enter value.

Use arcs to form the curved part of the "D" shape.

Push/Pull tool. It looks like a bow and arrow. Select it, then click the top right side and bottom right side of the "D" rectangle. When you move your mouse to the right of the rectangle, an arc will form. Click again to set that arc where you want it.

Go back to the toolbar and select the tool to the right of the Push/Pull tool. This is the Offset tool. It looks like an arc with a red arrow creating a larger copy of the arc. This is exactly what we are going to do. Click on the arc of the "D." Now move your mouse in toward the center of the "D" until you like where the second arc is. Click again to set it.

## Solid Skills

We covered a lot of new skills in this chapter. Let's take some time and make sure you've mastered them all. Can you alter the "3D" model you made? Try connecting the "3" and "D" together into a single, solid shape. Now try putting a hole through the middle of the solid. You already made a number and a letter—can you make more? How about the first letter of your name? For a real challenge, try spelling out your whole name in 3D shapes!

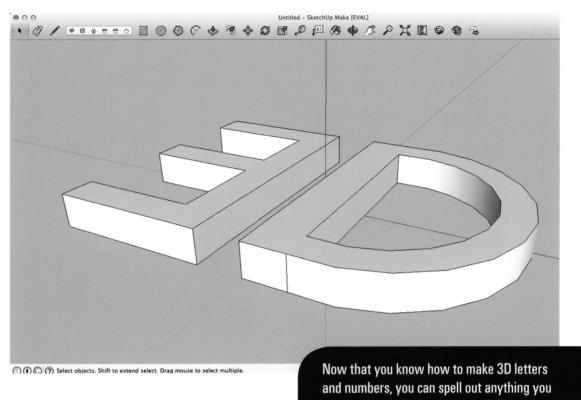

Select objects. Shift to extend select. Drag mouse to select multiple.

Now that you know how to make 3D letters and numbers, you can spell out anything you want to.

Once again, we must delete the lines between the arcs and rectangle of the "D." When you're done, there should be a "3" and a "D" filled with light gray. Now select the Push/Pull tool and pull the "3" and the "D" upward. Use the Orbit tool to change your view if needed. Holding shift as you pull the "3" and "D" will help you keep them the same height. Ta-da! You're finished!

Chapter 4

# What's Next?

Y ou've got a handle on the basics of curve modeling. There is a lot more to learn about 3D modeling, though. There are a ton of tools

Once you get good at using the right software, you can make 3D models of anything you can imagine.

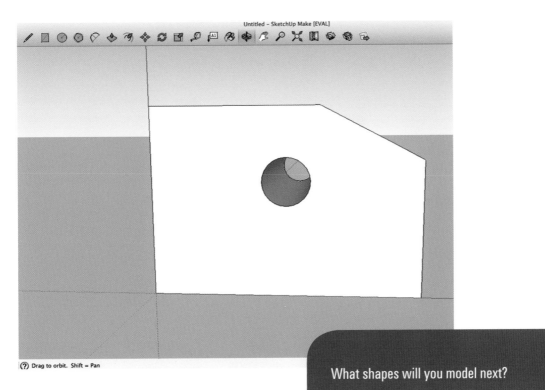

What shapes will you model next?

left to explore in SketchUp, not to mention entire
other templates. You can also find the Render tool
and make cool pictures of your models. Play around!
Experiment! Have fun! Make something completely
crazy! Can you build a model of a house? How about a
potato peeler?

Keep in mind that this is only one kind of
3D modeling and that all software is different. Most
3D modeling software is also very expensive.
Try out some free and simple ones to figure out if

you really want to dive deeper into 3D modeling. If you want to try polygonal modeling, ask an adult to help you download and install Blender (www.blender.org). Blender is a free polygonal modeling program that can be used for all kinds of applications. There are many guides on the Internet that will help you learn

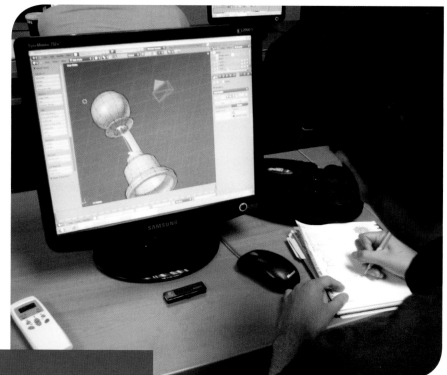

Try taking a class if you want to learn more about a specific type of 3D modeling software.

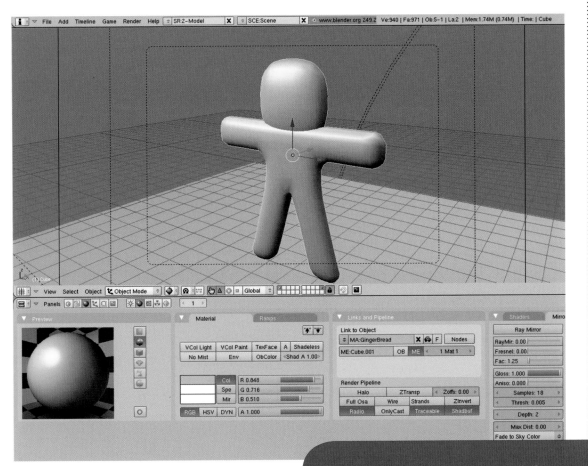

Blender is a good program to start with if you want to learn about polygonal modeling.

how to use it. There is currently no free digital sculpting software available, but perhaps there will be in the future.

As you practice modeling and learn more about different software, your skills will get better and better. Soon, you might be creating your own animated movies or modeling complex new inventions. You might even be able to turn your modeling skills into a career making video games or designing products. No matter what you end up doing, though, you're sure to have a great time!

## A Step Ahead

To make more complex models, you will need to learn some new concepts. Here are some things that might come in handy when working with SketchUp and other curve modeling software:

| | |
|---|---|
| Boolean | In polygonal and curve modeling, a boolean is when you take two objects and merge them together. Or, you use one object to take a bite out of the other. In SketchUp, you can do a boolean using the Outer Shell, Intersect, Union, Subtract, Trim, and Split tools. |
| Sweep | A sweep occurs when you take one shape, such as a square, and then push/pull it along a path, such as a circle. The result in this case would be a ring shape. In many 3D modeling programs, this is the best way to create new, complex shapes. SketchUp's sweep tool is called Follow Me. |

**A Step Ahead**

Colors and Textures

You have probably noticed that at first, the models you create are flat and colorless. You might want to spice up your creations. There are tools that allow you to add colors or give an object a different texture. You can even put an image on the surface of an object. In SketchUp, you can work with colors, textures, and images using the Colors tool.

# Glossary

**arc** (AHRK) a curved line between two points

**axes** (AK-seez) imaginary lines through the middle of an object

**makers** (MAY-kurz) people who invent or create things

**pan** (PAN) to move a camera over a wide area in order to display that area or follow an action

**polygonal** (puh-LIH-guh-nuhl) made of flat shapes that each have three or more sides, such as triangles or squares

**radius** (RAY-dee-uhs) a straight line drawn from the exact center of a circle to its edge

**renderings** (REN-dur-ingz) pictures or videos of a computer-generated 3D model

**template** (TEM-plit) document or pattern used to create similar documents

**underlying geometry** (UHN-dur-lye-ing jee-AH-muh-tree) the shapes, lines, and surfaces that make up an object's form

**zoom** (ZOOM) to adjust a camera lens so that the thing pictured appears farther away or close

# Find Out More

## BOOKS

O'Neill, Terence, and Josh Williams. *3D Printing*. Ann Arbor, MI: Cherry Lake Publishing, 2013.

Roslund, Samantha, and Emily Puckett Rodgers. *Makerspaces.* Ann Arbor, MI: Cherry Lake Publishing, 2014.

## WEB SITES

### Blender
*www.blender.org/*
Download and learn more about Blender.

### SketchUp
*www.sketchup.com/*
Download the SketchUp program and learn more about 3D modeling.

# Index

## About the Author

Theo Zizka is a recent graduate from the University of Michigan Stamps School of Art and Design and a program assistant for Michigan Makers, an after-school program for young makers. He aspires to be a full-time maker, designing products and making artwork.